Called to Compassion

A Retreat with
Saint Marguerite Bourgeoys

Louise Finn, CND

Cover Image
by Sr. Marguerite Garon, CND, 1977
(Number 493. C.N.D. Archives, Montreal)

We wish to thank the Knights of Columbus
for their generous grant
to the Congregation of Notre Dame
for help with the printing of this book.

ISBN # 978-0-615-20753-7
Printed in the United States of America

First Printing

In gratitude
to my family – loving and fun-loving,
and to the
Congregation of Notre Dame,
whose many Sisters and Associates
have blessed my life
with their support and friendship

Contents

'Saint Marguerite Bourgeoys'
by Mary Southard, CSJ, 1982

FOREWORD

SAINT MARGUERITE BOURGEOYS, WOMAN OF VISION

On October 31, 1982, Marguerite Bourgeoys, a French woman of the seventeenth century, was 'canonized,' that is, officially declared a saint by the church.

We may well ask, what can a person who lived more than three hundred years ago say to us today? In Marguerite's case, a great deal! She left her native France as a young single lay woman to join with other committed lay persons in a wonderful adventure. This small group of a few hundred—mostly men—crossed the ocean to build a community of faith and charity in a small outpost, Ville Marie (now Montreal), in New France. Today, in a world of global connections at every turn, we can still be challenged as Christians to abandon nationalistic goals and personal careers for the good of others in a distant land.

Marguerite committed herself to community building within a society and church which was itself not free from corruption or self-serving interests. Commitment is a challenge in every generation. When the media portray the many sins of our church today, the tendency is to equate the sins of the clergy or laity with the Body of Christ—to the exclusion of every other aspect of this Body.

However, we are more than our sins; we are also our dreams. Marguerite was well aware of the difficulties of trying to do something new among those who fear change: one person's vision can be a dangerous threat to others. Yet she dared to envision a new way of being Church. There is still a cry among us for this vision.

Marguerite lived in a fort in a small village but went beyond its borders to the Native People, teaching their children and, in a few cases, taking in their orphans. Today, walled neighborhoods have returned to our cities. Fear keeps many behind the tall brick ramparts. The challenge today, as in Marguerite's time, is to go beyond the walls to be with the 'others'—whoever they may be. Our walls in Texas and Arizona attempt to keep out the immigrant poor. Our faith challenges us to tackle the complexity of the immigration issue with openness and charity.

Marguerite gathered women around her and eventually formed a community, the Sisters of the Congregation of Notre Dame. At a time when women religious were cloistered, she dreamed of a group that would follow the journeying Mother of God who went off to visit her cousin Elizabeth as soon as she heard that this elderly cousin was pregnant. Between Marguerite's dream and its fulfillment were many years of difficult struggle, but Marguerite persevered. Although church authorities maintained that religious had to be cloistered, Marguerite continued the conversation about the possibility of another way.

Finally, when she was 78, her small group received permission to become the first non-cloistered religious congregation in North America. Patience with a slow moving Church is as necessary today as it was three hundred years ago. If it is the will of God, the dream will endure. In a culture of immediate gratification and instant communication, waiting has become a lost art. Marguerite could teach it to us.

Marguerite came to Canada to form a new Christian community and to teach the children, especially the girls, who at this time in history were not always educated. Today women and children account for 80% of those living in poverty. Half the world's children—one billion!—live in poverty. Millions of women spend several hours each day collecting water. In today's world, a saint who worked for and stood with both women and children is indeed contemporary.

In a throw-away climate that surrounds us at every level—from material things to personal relationships, a Congregation that endures for over three hundred years is a witness to the power of God alive and well in our midst. Saint Marguerite Bourgeoys has inspired women from all over the world to follow in her way of ministry. The first American to become a religious sister was Lydia Longley from Massachusetts, who joined the Congregation in 1699 during Marguerite's own lifetime. In the mid-nineteenth century slavery-days in this country, Eliza Healey, daughter of a slave woman, became a member of the Congregation.

Today there are members of the Congregation of Notre Dame—Our Lady's Congregation—from Belgium, Cameroon, Canada, Honduras, Guatemala, El Salvador, France, Japan and the United States. Moreover, over 900 Associates—women and men who wish to be part of our outreach to others in the spirit of Mary's Visitation to Elizabeth—now join us in ministering to the people in these countries.

Marguerite is surely a Woman of Vision for us today. May these words taken from and inspired by her writings help you to see other, new ways of living your Christian life in our challenging world.

Patricia McCarthy, CND

'Marguerite Bourgeoys'
by Sr. Cecile Marois, CND, 1914 - 1979
(Number 1424. C.N.D. Archives, Montreal)

xii

Part One

INTRODUCTION

About This Retreat

Called to Compassion . . . Perhaps as you looked at the title of this book, you wondered, "Who is called to compassion?" Or "Just what is this compassion?"

> **compassion** – [< Lat. cum = with + pati = to feel, suffer] – the capacity to feel another's pain and the desire to respond to it in a practical way

Throughout the centuries we see this compassion lived out in the lives of the saints, both the "official"—Vincent de Paul, Marguerite Bourgeoys, Damien the Leper, and the "unofficial"—Mohandas Gandhi, Dorothy Day. We see it too in coworkers and neighbors who are quick to respond kindly to the needs and feelings of others.

So **who** are "**called to compassion**"? Are some people born to it, and others called to it?

Scripture reminds us that God is love" (1 Jn 4:8). Surely then, this same God is also compassion—the limitless capacity to feel and respond to the tremendous suffering in our world, both in those we know personally and in those whose tearful faces are known to us only through the media.

"You have made us for Yourself, O God, and our hearts are restless until we rest in You." (Saint Augustine). If we wish to rest in God, we are called to be fully human! Love and compassion are a vital part of being truly human. So who are called to compassion? Every human being on the planet, all of us—in our own time, and in our own way, great or small.

Are you a traditional Christian facing the daily tensions of this confusing world? A Catholic looking for a way to center your life more fully in God? A former Catholic wondering if you are missing something important? A 'seeker' searching to deepen your relationship with God, to integrate this relationship into your life? This book may help you find these answers. It is an invitation to have as your prayer-mentor and guide one of the most powerful, wise and appealing women in our faith tradition.

In her humanness and holiness, Marguerite Bourgeoys can help you grow in self-knowledge, discernment of God's desires for your life, and maturity in the Spirit. Your friendship with Marguerite will feed your soul with wisdom and peace, as she brings forth from her storeroom "what is new and old."

Although the format of this book is "seven days of prayer" (traditionally called a retreat), it may be adapted to different schedules and different purposes. The reflection questions and closing prayer at the end of each day may help you see Marguerite in your own geographical, historical and cultural setting. They may also challenge and guide you in integrating the day's theme into your daily life.

The retreat days need not be consecutive, nor is anyone expected to spend 24 hours in non-stop prayer! So, in between the prayer-periods, what do you do? If you're at home, perhaps some household chores or yard-work—physical exercise is helpful to prayer, or some creative handicrafts—sewing, knitting, carpentry, sketching—"whatever." It might also be wise to skip TV, chatty phone-calls and non-urgent emails. If possible, replace them with rest, walking, or quiet reading, so that you will return to your next prayer-period refreshed and ready to meet God!

You are probably aware that the real mentor-director of everyone who makes a retreat is the Holy Spirit. However, for more than three hundred years Marguerite's words and spirit have spoken to thousands who sought to strengthen and deepen their relationship with God. So with her as your guide, you are traveling in good company. Moreover, Marguerite is not only praying with you during these days, but her prayers for you have no doubt already helped you decide to take this extra time for prayer.

In 1976 the English translation of Marguerite's writings was published. Such a book—nearly 150 pages of text, authenticated by historians, is a small miracle coming as it does from a world in which fires frequently destroyed whole buildings and all their treasures. As a person of the seventeenth century, Marguerite reflects in her writings the culture, the spirituality and the language of her time. Yet, since human nature is the same in every age, very little adaptation is necessary for us to accept most of her suggestions and advice.

What is necessary for these pages, however, is a broader interpretation of her words, since her purpose in writing was to help the sisters of the congregation which she had founded. Wherever possible I have used Marguerite's own words and put them in italics. In integrating them into this format, I have tried to be faithful to her spirit, in the context of the themes that emerged from her writings.

The actual text, therefore, is written as if spoken by Saint Marguerite herself. As you read "her" suggestions for each day's prayer periods, you may then use whatever prayer forms are most helpful to you—contemplation, meditation, journaling, centering prayer, meditative reading, or combinations of these. If the opening prayer of each day expands into your entire prayer period, fine! Let its words (or others of your choice) stay in your mind and heart until they are yours. At the end of each day's prayer suggestions, I have added a poem (my own) related to one aspect of the day's theme. This poem may provide another dimension, other insights. If so, fine. If, however, you find it does not help you, ignore it—or improve it! In fact, during these precious days, use whatever may help you to grow in grateful awareness of God's loving presence and passionate, compassionate, unconditional love!

On a more personal note I wish to add that in August, 2000 Sister Lorraine Caza, our Congregation Leader at the time, came to Ngaoundéré, Cameroon, to give a retreat to the sisters in the area. Some of her insights are within these pages, like jewels sparkling on a sandy beach. We treasured them, especially since we knew that she herself lives her words to others. I am deeply grateful to her for all she shared with us during that beautiful week, and for her exhortation to me that I undertake this project. I pray that her confidence was not misplaced.

I wish to express my gratitude to those who cheered me on along the way, especially to Sister Theresa Galvan, who read the original draft of this manuscript. Her careful critique and encouragement were most helpful. Sisters Patricia Simpson and Joan Foliot also offered many valuable suggestions and corrections. I truly appreciated their caring and insightful recommendations.

Many friends and colleagues have also helped to make the rough ways smooth at various stages of the journey: my sister Martha ("Mickie") Andres, Fr. Philip Fischer, SJ, Julie Fontaine (CND Archivist), Renee Hager (Secretary Extraordinaire!), Janet Kraus, Jim Messina, Dori Reidy and Mary Southard, CSJ. My CND Sisters also performed small miracles on my behalf: Martha Bowes, Joann Compagno, Peggy Doyle, Natalie Gannon, Betty King, Alyn Larson, Patricia McCarthy, Joyce Roberts and Jane Ann Scanlon. My sincere thanks to each!

My gratitude, of course, goes mostly to Marguerite Bourgeoys. May I dare to speak, then, for both her and myself? We urge you to feel perfectly free to draw on Scripture, art, literature, music, psychology and contemporary events to make these pages more intimate for you. Remember, what you will read here is only part of the retreat's content. You (and God) supply the rest! After—or during—the retreat, you may wish to discuss with another visible mentor or prayer-partner some of your questions, desires, doubts and decisions—seeds that the Spirit has planted in your heart.

You may also wish to adapt the material to the number of prayer periods in **your** daily plan, staying with one or another for several periods, or repeating one, especially if it has been either very peaceful or very disturbing. Listen to your body too, taking sufficient time for exercise and rest. As Marguerite would say, *God is pleased with our desires and efforts*, so try to avoid judging your prayer. If other commitments limit your retreat days to fewer than seven—for example, to three, or even to one, enjoy whatever time you can spend with God in this special way. God's power is not subject to our timelines, so relax in God's timeless omnipotence!

In her opening conference Sister Lorraine spoke of a retreat as 'an adventure in faith.' Others sometimes refer to a retreat as 'a vacation with God.' Either way, may each of your prayer sessions begin with a smile on your face and a song in your heart!

Engraving for Faillon's biography of Marguerite Bourgeoys, 1853, by Massard (Marguerite Bourgeoys Museum, Montreal)

About Marguerite,
Your Retreat Director

Saint Marguerite Bourgeoys—surely the name evokes several images: pioneer woman, founder of the Congregation of Notre Dame, co-founder of the city of Montreal. Even during her lifetime she was called "Mother of the Colony"! Although her life spanned most of the seventeenth century, it was only in 1982 that she was canonized, that is, officially declared a saint by the church. But behind these few historical facts lies an amazing story of a dynamic and deeply spiritual woman.

In her memoirs Marguerite speaks of a retreat she made to thank God for her baptism and other graces of her life. Let us travel back in time to 1698, less than two years before she died, as she reviewed her life in grateful prayer. What might have been her thoughts as she looked back over her 78 years?

Being a practical and methodical woman, she began at the beginning, April 17, 1620. It was on Good Friday that she had been taken—not yet one day old!—to the parish church to be baptized. The ceremony had been simple and subdued, but afterwards the five Bourgeoys children had given their baby sister an exuberant homecoming. Her father was a master candle maker in the city of Troyes, France, as it recovered from the devastation of the religious wars and political intrigues that had splintered Europe for nearly a century. For the time being, business was brisk—a blessing indeed, with six more children arriving after Marguerite. Despite the memory of four tiny graves, she remembered a cheerful home filled with contented children and loving parents. Then another poignant memory: her mother's death when she herself was eighteen. During the years that followed, she had helped her older sister care for the three little ones who had survived infancy.

With such a lively trio already, why not add a few more? When the neighbors' children found out that Marguerite would tell them Bible stories, they came flocking! Throughout the city's churches, images of Jesus, Mary and the saints peopled the walls and windows. Through Marguerite, these statues and paintings came to life for her young "pupils."

Some of her friends urged her to join the "extern congregation," a group of young women that acted as an outreach for the local cloistered Sisters of Notre Dame. They could use her wholesome energy to enliven their meetings and help with the work among the poor families. But then she considered their rule that forbade showy lace or fancy styles—such fussy simplicity! Marguerite declined.

Rosary Sunday, 1640—the most beautiful memory of all! She was twenty, an age when several of her sisters had married, and most young women were making life decisions. As she walked in the parish procession, she looked up at the stone statue above the church entrance. For a few moments, Mary's gaze met hers, and Marguerite felt herself completely changed. Our Lady had transformed her immaturity, without sacrificing the natural attractiveness of her personality. It was at that moment, she recalled, that she had truly given herself to God. And she knew too that with

Our Lady's smile, the seed of the Congregation had actually been planted in her heart by Mary herself.

Although even as a young woman Marguerite had a healthy distrust of conspicuous piety, she joined the extern group. The young women met regularly in the convent parlor to pray together and to plan for their projects, especially teaching the poor. They knew that the wealthy had tutors, and middle-class children learned from religious such as the cloistered Benedictines, but for the poor, schools were nonexistent. Gratefully she accepted the teacher training that the cloistered Notre Dame Sisters offered her, using it well with the growing number of young women in the group and with the children whom they taught.

But soon she felt drawn to give herself to God more deeply, more fully. Having sought the advice of a priest who knew her well, she asked to be admitted to the Carmelite Sisters. How baffled she was at their refusal! What would her life have been like, she mused, if they had said yes? And what if her first attempt to form a religious community in Troyes had succeeded? God certainly let her know that this plan was not to be, with the death of one companion and the departure of the other! Nor did her attempts to enter other cloistered communities succeed. Perhaps these failures deepened her desire to follow Mary, the "Journeying Virgin-Mother," who rose with haste to visit Elizabeth and went wherever she was needed to bring Christ to others.

By now Marguerite was 33. Well aware that most people of her time did not live beyond 45, she felt her life was slipping away. What did God want of her? Through a very unusual meeting, God let her know. Monsieur de Maisonneuve . . . the memory of this lifelong friend and co-worker warmed her heart! As the one in charge of the new

11

French colony in Canada, he had arrived in Troyes looking for someone to return with him to the settlement to be the teacher there. When Marguerite was recommended for this position, she had sensed that this was the true answer to her long search for God's designs on her life. Her prayers and investigations further strengthened this conviction, and she prepared to go.

Shortly before they were to embark, however, the Carmelites sent word to Marguerite that she could now join them. Was she being unwise in turning them down and planning to make this dangerous voyage, as almost everyone was warning her? Torn with anxiety, she turned to Mary for her answer. Once again her trust was rewarded with Our Lady's clear assurance: "Go, I will never abandon you!" In peace, she continued her journey to New France.

But what a voyage! Two months on a plague-infested ship, tending the fever-ridden, comforting the dying, encouraging the fearful! When they finally sailed up the Saint Lawrence to Ville Marie (later called Montreal), such a welcome sight! Pitiful as it was, the sight of the wooden stockade and its little houses nourished her hope that she would soon be a teacher again.

After nearly five years of helping the settlers in numerous other ways, Marguerite was finally able to begin classes with the nine children who had survived the cold winters. A stone stable became their first schoolhouse, while the loft above served as living quarters for Marguerite and her helper.

With relief she recalled her voyage back to France that same year, 1658. After three long months of seemingly endless seas, she came to a far deeper appreciation of the "ocean of God's mercy," and she later succeeded in bringing

12

back four young women to help her in her new work. All she could promise them was bread and soup, but they had sensed her enthusiasm and had decided to come!

Other young faces passed before Marguerite's inner vision. The "King's Wards," orphan-girls sent to become wives of the settlers. . . . How could she ever forget them? Had she not welcomed them, provided a home and a special home-makers' school for them, and even moved in with them at the cost of leaving her co-workers? More than once she had helped in the selection of just the right husband for one of them, and often the young brides had later turned to her in this harsh land as to a mother.

Within a few years Marguerite had been able to move back with her sisters, as her companions were now called. Those were busy days—and nights too, for when their teaching day was over, in order to support themselves they would tend the farm and sew for the colonists. And Bishop Laval was urging her to expand their work throughout the entire colony of New France. She could not refuse, for people needed to learn, and there was no one else to go to them. Making the rounds of all the settlements in the growing diocese was no easy trek, but they had managed.

That next journey in 1670 . . . Marguerite had realized that she would soon need the King's authorization for her group to teach in the colony; once again she faced the long ocean voyage, but this time her small parcel of luggage was left behind! Since she was the only woman on board, she made do with some coarse hemp and a coil of rope—and, thank God, the trip had lasted only 31 days. On her return, she had brought six more helpers. Five years later Bishop Laval was to recognize the small group of ten as a religious community within his diocese.

That year, 1676, they had opened a school for the Algonquin children in the Indian village close to Ville Marie. To make them feel more at home, the two sisters had even lived and taught in a small bark hut. What a blessing when two young Native women (one a Mohawk and the other a Huron) later joined the Congregation and went to the village to teach the people!

Processions and pilgrimages—these were as important to the rhythm of the colony as teaching and growing crops. Yes, somehow the colonists had found time to help construct Notre Dame de Bon Secours—that sturdy church built in Mary's honor. Marguerite had sometimes wondered if this project she had started would ever be finished: more than twenty years elapsed before it had finally been completed. She dreamed of the distant day when the statue of Our Lady of Good Help would perhaps stand like a beacon on its dome to welcome all who sailed into the harbor. But for now she knew that surely Mary was watching over the growing settlement.

The following year, back to France—a strange journey, for Bishop Laval, who had previously been so supportive of her work, now sent word to Marguerite that she was not to bring back even one recruit! It was after that, she recalled gratefully, that instead, young Canadian women began to join their ranks.

At least she had succeeded in her second purpose for that trip, namely, to study the Rules of other religious communities in preparation for writing her own. Lovingly her eyes rested on the small book in her lap—the "Rule," whose words embodied her vision of their new congregation. Until the community had its Rule in writing, it could not be officially approved by the church. And above all, Marguerite wished to serve this church. But what a long delay before approval was granted! She had been convinced that the sisters must remain uncloistered if they were to follow Mary in her going out to others, while church authorities seemed just as certain that "real religious" must be cloistered.

The bishop had listened at last. Just a few months before her retreat, 24 sisters had publicly pronounced their vows, promising to follow in the footsteps of Mary in carrying God to those whom they served. On that solemn occasion Marguerite had chosen as her religious name, Sister Marguerite of the Blessed Sacrament. Through the Eucharist, the all-encompassing mystery of Christ's redemptive love, she and her sisters drew strength to combat the forces of ignorance that paralyzed and misdirected so many people. She could find no words to thank God for his sacramental presence in her home, in her life!

Several months after this retreat, Marguerite learned of the critical illness of the young sister in charge of the novices. She asked God to take her life instead, and God accepted her offering. On January 12, 1700, after ten days of intense suffering, she died peacefully, confident that Mary would keep her promise not to abandon her on her final journey.

Over the centuries her work lived on and grew. Today more than 1200 sisters of her congregation are engaged in educational ministries in Canada, the United States, Japan, Central America, Cameroon and France. They still try to live in the spirit of Mary's Visitation, sometimes traveling great psychological distances to meet others wherever they are. Since 1982 Marguerite has been recognized as a saint, a person who loved God and others in ordinary ways but to an extraordinary degree.

Looking back, we see Marguerite Bourgeoys not only as a woman of her time, but ahead of her time and for our own time. Her understanding of Mary's role in the early church strengthened her vision of women's role in the church of her day. The importance she gave to family life in the colony finds echoes in today's ministries. Like so many good people today, she opened her home to refugees from violence and poverty. Patiently, persistently, she worked "through the system," both political and ecclesiastical. Despite her reticence concerning her personal spiritual experiences, she is now recognized as one of the mystics of the church. In her thirst for justice, she opened schools for the poor, to teach them what they needed to know in order to live more fully human lives.

But most of all, we see Marguerite as a practical, compassionate woman of faith, whose genuine kindness we can try to imitate. Like Jesus in the Gospels, she felt for others in their sufferings, and did whatever she could to alleviate these sufferings, to respond to these needs. We too are encouraged to trust, as she did, in the mercy of our God and in Mary's help, as we take the creative risks called for in our daily journey through this challenging world.

"I used to do sewing and in payment,
would ask for a day's work" (on Bon Secours Chapel).
Writings of Marguerite Bourgeoys, p. 113
CND Artists' Series, 1950
(Marguerite Bourgeoys Museum, Montreal)

17

Part Two

Day 1

Walking with Mary,
Woman of Faith

Mary's song of gratitude in Luke 1 echoes that of Hannah, another mother, as it poured forth spontaneously from her lips. And your own Magnificat? How would you express your gratitude for God's work in you? Use your own words, your own life experiences to express your gratitude. Below is one way of doing this, but remember, your **own** way is best for **you**!

OPENING PRAYER

"The Almighty works marvels for me; holy is his name!"
(Lk 1:49)

You, O God,
are the song we sing
as we try by our lives
to mirror your mercy,
to struggle for justice,
to accept our own weakness
and act with your strength.

May we find our deepest joy
in serving others,
in holding out our emptiness
for you to fill,
in caring for our small portion
of your beckoning vineyard!

~~~~~ I ~~~~~

Who is Mary for you? Is her place in your life based on sound theology but lacking in warmth? Perhaps my own was a bit like this before I saw her smile during that procession on Rosary Sunday when I was twenty. Did she really smile? Or did I just open the eyes of my heart to see her beauty? In any case, I know she changed my life! Or perhaps you have grown up close to her as to an ideal mother, knowing the marvels our God has done for her!

*The Blessed Virgin was a child of prayer, offered to God from her birth. When her Son called the Apostles to build the church, she helped them to recognize the designs of their Master, all of whose words she kept in her heart. She followed him everywhere, even to the foot of the Cross, where she was given as mother to Saint John and in him to all Christians. *

She sustained the church until the descent of the Holy Spirit. She was mother and teacher to the new-born Church, which she formed and instructed in all kinds of good by her words and by her example. In so many ways, Mary is like living water, crystal clear, springing up from the fountains of the Savior and refreshing all who come to it!*

21

Speak to Mary about your desire to understand her better, to become more like her, to learn to live your yes as she did, to entrust yourself and your loved ones to her motherly care, now and always.

* Remember that each day's reflections are written as if Marguerite is "speaking" to you, and that the words *in italics* are taken directly from *The Writings of Saint Marguerite Bourgeoys.*

~~~~~ **II** ~~~~~

Recall the first two chapters of Luke's gospel, the stories that tell us about Mary's part in the Incarnation. Look carefully at Mary as the story unfolds:

Mary listens as God's messenger asks her permission to allow God to become human through the flesh of her own body.

Mary journeys to visit her elderly cousin, to help her in her need and to share with her the incredible joy that unites them.

Mary brings forth her Son in an animals' shelter and listens to the strange story of the shepherds who come to see him.

Mary presents her baby in obedience to God's law and listens to Simeon's words, words that speak of her Son as the Savior of the world, and of the sword that will pierce her own soul.

Mary and Joseph find the boy Jesus "at home in his Father's house," and listen to his words that remind them of who he is, for them and for us.

In each of these scenes, we see Mary listening carefully to someone, and learning from that person what God wanted her to hear at that moment. Each word drew her further from her own dreams and more deeply into God's truth, God's will.

Reread these passages (Lk 1-2) and listen to the same words that Mary heard. Ponder these words with her. Feel the questions, the joys, the wonder, the pain in her heart.

"The Almighty works marvels for me; holy is his name!" Talk with Mary about the many marvels that God did for her, in her, through her. Rejoice with her for each of them! You might wish to do this by saying the rosary. *The rosary is the time to thank God for favors he granted the Blessed Virgin and to acknowledge her as our mother and our all, after God.* Besides praying the usual fifteen mysteries that I used to pray, you now have the lovely Luminous Mysteries too. And do not hesitate to replace any of these at times with other events in the life of Jesus and Mary, for example, events in the gospel of the day.

~~~~~ **III** ~~~~~

Reread the story of Cana (Jn 2:1-11), and listen to her prayer on behalf of the young couple: "They have no more wine." So simple, direct, urgent! Can we too pray with this compassion for a world in need of the wine of truth, of honesty, of respect, of peace? Listen to her words, her last recorded message in the gospels: "Whatever he tells you to do, do it." Could anything be more clear?

I always felt that besides all the other gifts of my life, I had *still another recourse which the merciful God was kind enough to give me: the help of the Blessed Virgin. If I am the object of God's mercy, I am at the same time a proof of her help.*

While I was still struggling with the decision to come to Montreal—the decision which led me to my life's work for the church and for our people, she gave me her special reassurance, *"Go, I will never abandon you." This gave me great courage.* Her words echoed those of her Son to us, "Behold, I am with you all days . . . ." As I look back on my life, I see more clearly how Mary kept her promise, and how her Son kept his. Both were with me every step of my journey.

Perhaps you too can look back on some of the "crises" in your own life—a crisis of faith, of health, of hope in others or in yourself, even a crisis of the very will to keep on trying. Somehow, you survived, and endured, and gained some degree of victory. This "somehow" was God's grace, Mary's help. As you allow these events to pass through the corridors of your memory—limping, or marching, or perhaps dancing—be grateful. They were the channels of great grace.

~~~~~**IV** ~~~~~

Mary's "Go, I will never abandon you" sustained and comforted me. I wonder, however, if Mary were to speak to each of us today, if her words would not be a little different. People seem to have the courage to go—to go here and there, to travel great distances both geographic and psychological, to journey with people in need of their help.

But do we also need the courage to let go? Would Mary perhaps say to us, "Learn to let go. I will never abandon you"?

Do we need to learn to let go of our doubts about God's care for us, for everyone in our world?

-- to let go of our need to feel important in others' eyes?

-- of our desire to be served as soon as we make a request?

-- of our lack of faith in the power of prayer, the prayer of the church, and our own?

-- of our blindness to so many blessings every day of our life?

-- of our lack of sensitivity to others' struggle and pain?

-- of our tendency to put our own agenda above others' real needs?

What gifts does Mary want to give you? How will you respond? As you ponder these questions, be real. Be yourself, your true self, but your best self—the self you have brought to these precious days of retreat!

CLOSING PRAYER

Mary will surely be with you during this special time with her Son. And so we pray...

To Mary Journeying

"For all your ways are beautiful . . ."

Be with us in the morning
As with joyful hearts we travel
to carry Christ within us
in silence and in song.

Be with us as we labor
on the hills and in the valleys
with your care and with your mercy
to all within our world.

And when evening shadows lengthen,
be our strength as still we journey
to our God whose arms await us
in the darkness of your peace.

*"The Blessed Virgin ... never excused herself from any
journey on which there was good to be done...."*
(Writings of Marguerite Bourgeoys, p. 50)
CND Artists' Series, 1942
by Sr. St. Marthe-de-Béthanie Dufresne
(Marguerite Bourgeoys Museum, Montreal)

Day 2

Rekindling the Fire

Let us begin this day by choosing a psalm, praying it slowly, reverently, remembering that it contains God's own words, prayed by countless holy people over the centuries. You might wish to select one or more of the following: Psalm 8, 19, 62, 84, 92, 100, 138.

OPENING PRAYER

"You have not chosen me.
No, I have chosen you." (Jn 15:16)

My dear and wonderful God, thank you for choosing me. . .
   . . . for choosing me to be born as a human being, able to know you, to respond to your words, your call, your passionate longing to give me yourself, to be my very life!
   . . . for choosing me to be a Christian, a follower of your Son, a member of his church, with its human failings and glorious role in our world!
   . . . for choosing me not because I am worthy or better than others who do not know you, but simply because you love me!
   . . . for choosing me from all eternity to be your daughter/son, part of your family, your messenger to others!

. . . for choosing me to make this retreat, for giving me the desire and the time to be with you in a special way these days, listening to you and speaking my own faltering response!

Thank you, God, for choosing me.

~~~~~ **I** ~~~~~

As you know, my earthly journey ended more than three hundred years ago. Yet in so many ways your life is like mine. Human nature is the same in every century, and our gracious God is ever-loving, infinitely merciful, inviting each of us to holiness. But do you sometimes feel that holiness is reserved for special people, perhaps people such as cloistered religious? With your constant stream of distractions during prayer and failings outside of prayer, you ask, is there any use in continuing to strive for holiness? But let's look again. We have in Mary not only a mother but also a model. Note well: *The Blessed Virgin was never cloistered. She did indeed withdraw into an interior solitude, but she never excused herself from any journey on which there was good to be done or some work of charity to be performed. We wish to follow her in some way.*

Surely you are already trying to do this, since you have scheduled this period of retreat so you too can "*withdraw into an interior solitude.*" You have taken the first step—or rather, you have responded to God's invitation to come aside and rest awhile.

The next step, then, is to listen attentively to God's voice. How do we do this? *God speaks to us through preachers and through readings, by all his creatures and by his precepts.* So often both in prayer and in conversation,

29

we only "half-listen," filtering out what we prefer not to hear, or merely pretending to be attentive. Yet listening is surely the most basic aspect of good communication. Perhaps God will speak to you during this retreat in a way you least expect. "He does not cry out . . ." (Is 42:8), so pray for the grace to listen well!

~~~~~ **II** ~~~~~

Listen for God's voice especially in quiet prayer. *Prayer without attention is of no use or of very little use; we must pay attention to what we ask, to what we promise and to what we ought to do for God. Unless prayer arises from the heart which ought to be its center, it is no more than a fruitless dream. Prayer ought to carry over into our words, our thoughts and our actions!*

Would you like to be on fire with love for God and others? Or are you a bit afraid of the idea, feeling it might be presumptuous to have such a desire? *It seems to me that we are charcoal ready to be kindled, and that Holy Communion is entirely suited to set us on fire! But when this charcoal is kindled only on the surface, as soon as it is set aside it is extinguished. On the contrary, that which is fired all the way to the center is not extinguished, but is consumed.*

Since the Eucharist is Christ's perfect Sacrifice, perhaps you would be wise to renew and deepen your faith in this mystery by pondering Jesus' words in John 6, especially verses 47-58. Remember, this Living Bread which unites us to our God is the Risen Christ, the same food that sustained the martyrs throughout the ages, right down to those of today.

"Greater love than this no one has . . . ." What better way to rekindle the fire of your love for God than to pray on Christ's passion? I used to tell the sisters that *they should have no more frequent subject for their meditations than the sufferings of the passion.* Spend a few quiet moments just gazing at your crucifix, or holding it in your hands. Try to realize that this body was that of a human being, the sinless God-man—all-powerful, all-loving, who ached with sadness for our pain, who gave his life because he loved us more than we can imagine. Let your heart respond to this love in simple words, perhaps repeating the same sentence or phrase for an entire prayer period.

~~~~~ **IV** ~~~~~

You may wish to turn to your favorite Scripture passages. My own suggestions might be of help:

"'Where do you live, Lord?' 'Come and see.'" (Jn 1:38-39)

"'Lord, if it's really you, bid me to come to you upon the waters.' And Jesus said, 'Come.'" (Mt 14:28-29)

"Come to me all who labor and are weary, and I will give you rest." (Mt 11:28)

Listen to Jesus speaking these words to you. What are your feelings now? Jesus is waiting for you to pour them out, just as they are. As you look into Jesus' eyes, ask yourself:

Why am I making this retreat?
How have I come to this point in my journey?
What graces do I want to pray for, for myself and for
    others?

Don't rush. Surprise yourself with the unexpected
honesty of your responses. Watch Jesus smile. Smile with
him. Relax. Take a walk. Pause reverently before a bush,
or a tree. Look—really look!—at a flower, a bird, a bug, a
cloud. Take a nap, or a swim, or both! Dance! Unwind!

Come!

Come, you say,
        your voice clear despite
        the wind, the slapping waves.
My hands grip the rough wood.
My legs, limp, yet rigid.
My throat too dry to utter one sound.
Fears paralyze my will. No, not fear,
        but wisdom—certain, strong!

Only a madman would heed
        a call to perish.
Only a fool would follow
        such a command.

Closer, your voice is closer.
Again, the same word: Come.
Your eyes meet mine.

Only for you will I leave this
small bark,
tossed and turning, yet far
more safe than churning water!

Only for you, God of madmen
and holy fools.
Only for you, Savior who
speaks my name.

CLOSING PRAYER

Our Lord and God! You are worthy to receive
glory, honor and power!
For you created all things, and by your will
they were given existence and life! (Rev 4:11)

Day 3

The Good Seed

Besides the Eucharist, another source of strength and light for our journey is Scripture, God's Word to us. As we begin this day, simply hold your Bible for a few minutes, reverently and gratefully.

OPENING PRAYER

"And the one who received the seed in rich soil is the person who hears the word and understands it; this person yields a harvest and produces now a hundredfold, now sixty, now thirty." (Mt 13:23)

My wise and loving God, thank you for giving us your Word to nourish our minds and hearts with your truth!

Help me to hear your Word with open ears, to read and ponder your Word with clear eyes and a listening heart.

Thank you for the many times you have touched my spirit through Scripture with just the right word, a word of comfort or caution or challenge—when I was ready to receive it. Ready my heart with your grace!

Did you read the rest of the parable about the farmer sowing his seed? Good, because Jesus' words are so much more important than mine! Do you recognize yourself among the types of soil where the seeds fell? Perhaps you are the rich soil, but like most good people, your harvest is not quite up to one hundred percent.

If ever you have planted a garden (or watched someone who did), you are aware of the many problems facing the gardener. Not only do the seeds need rich soil, but also moisture and sunlight. Sometimes a wire fence is necessary to keep out the predators, large and small, that would destroy the young plants before the harvest. But a thick wall instead of a fence might prevent that fine morning sun from warming the tender shoots.

Yes, *the Word of God is the good seed, but the person who wishes to remain in his/her own blindness raises a high wall which the sun cannot penetrate, and nothing is produced.* Ask yourself if you have raised such a wall. It might be an attitude of 'busy-ness'—even in prayer, a habit of being over-extended or of not getting enough rest, an unwillingness to forgive yourself or others, a lack of trust in God's love. Ask God to tear down this barricade to growth and allow the Spirit's seed to flourish in the warmth of your heart.

~~~~~ II ~~~~~

Sometimes we resort to a small box on a window sill for our garden, but if we are not open to others—their needs, their ideas, their culture, our blinders act like *the shutters of closed windows.* (In my day, shutters were functional, not ornamental as they are now.) *Other small faults which we think do not need to be corrected are like panes of glass,* perhaps not too clean. *And since the sun does not come straight down on the earth, it does not produce any flowers. But when the heart is open to the sun of grace, we see flowers blossom in their fragrance.* The good seed has come to fruition.

God in his wisdom has made us co-creators with him. Parents and teachers, poets and artists, peacemakers gardeners, nurses, technicians—all, all!—are collaborators with God to continue and complete creation. Having received the good seed into our hearts, we must try to live its message as well as we can. Such is the gift, the glorious call to be fully human!

~~~~~ **III** ~~~~~

We know that saints of all ages have come to know and love God more deeply by studying, pondering, and praying the Scriptures. In the gospels we also see Jesus or his mother referring to passages in the Hebrew Scriptures, which they probably knew by heart. For example, Mary's Magnificat is largely a paraphrase of Hannah's gratitude for the birth of her son Samuel (1 Sam 2:1-10).

Perhaps you might choose several psalms, praying them as Jesus might have prayed them to his Father. Ask that you might enter into the feelings of his heart as he prayed these same words— feelings of awe, of gratitude, of desire, of joy, of sorrow for the sufferings of humankind and for the vengeance expressed by the psalmist. One or more of the following might be helpful: Psalm 23, 42, 113, 121, 148.

Even if you have had no opportunity to study the Bible through courses or lectures, there are so many other ways to grow in understanding of Scripture. No matter what you resolve to do, be sure to take time to sit with God's word and cooperate with the sun of his grace. Gradually your harvest will increase, "sixty, eighty, a hundredfold"—but let's leave the mathematics to God!

Perhaps we could also ask for the great grace to be fully alive in every part of our being. Are we filled with quiet energy, yet able to relax in leisure, to rest in prayer? Are we ready to try different modes of thinking and acting, yet able to stick with tedious tasks? Are we willing to try new solutions to new struggles or to persistent problems? Are we, like Jesus in the gospels, at home with intense emotions—sadness at death and impending disaster, anger at desecration of holy places and cruelty towards human weakness, admiration for a widow's generosity and an unbeliever's faith, burning desire to give ourselves to nourish others' hunger?

Seeds must die if they are to give life. So, with God's grace, while holding fast to all that is alive within us, might we break out of our encrusted habits, our worn-out ways!

The Seed

Prophets heard your silent voice
    and spoke your mighty words.
Parchments told your story, your call,
    held safe your message of mercy.

Scribes pondered, proclaimed, explained
            meanings behind meanings, beyond.
But that was not enough for love,
            for infinite Love.

In dark of earth you reached
            down, further down,
thirsting for moisture, nurture,
            fathering all that is—yet son!

Mist, dew, desire drew you forth:
            a tiny shoot, fragile-firm.
In time came stem and leaves,
            slender, supple strength.

Burgeoning buds quietly opened—
            sun-warmed, breeze-bent,
ripening grain, banquet of gold:
            And the Word was made flesh!

CLOSING PRAYER

How sweet is the taste of your instructions —
            sweeter even than honey.
Your word is a lamp to guide me and a light for my path.
Accept my prayer of thanks, O Lord, and teach me your
            commands.
(Ps. 103, 105, 108, 119)

'Pseudo-Le Ber'
Artist & date unknown
Copy by Jori Smith-Palardi, 1963.
(Margaret Bourgeoys Museum, Montreal)

Day 4

Attentive to Our Guest

Today let us look at one of the most important mysteries of our faith: God dwelling within our hearts. In order to grasp this mystery more fully, let us ask Jesus to enlighten our limited human minds with his own unfailing light.

OPENING PRAYER

"I am the Light of the world.
The one who follows me will have the light of life
and will never walk in darkness."
(Jn 8:12)

All-powerful and merciful God, thank you for the gift of light! Even if it is only a candle flickering in the darkness, it can be enough for what I need to do. You are always enough. No matter what else I may want, you are all I truly need.

Sometimes you are like a flashlight with its strong beam keeping my steps safe in the dark around me. Thank you.

After a moonless, starless night, you flood my world with the splendor of dawn. Once again I see clearly the gifts that surround me—if the eyes of my heart are truly open. Thank you for the bright rays of light in my life.

At the close of each day, you withdraw the fullness of light gently, slowly, predictably. Sometimes you paint the sky with splashes of color to prepare us to renew our energies in peaceful sleep. Thank you.

Thank you for lighting my path with safety, clarity and beauty. Help me today to look honestly at the ways in which I sometimes prefer to walk in darkness.

~~~~~ I ~~~~~

Life—anyone's life—is a series of ordinary days and ordinary events, punctuated at times by the extraordinary. With God's help each of us is slowly weaving all the strands of our lives into a tapestry, to be finished only with our last breath. How do we make this tapestry a true work of art? *The rule for everyone is the one God gave from the creation of the world: "You shall love God with all your heart and your neighbor as yourself."*

Are these words so familiar that they have lost their power to startle you? Pause and listen again to each phrase. Ask to hear them as if for the first time. Then ask yourself:

What are my priorities, the most important things in each day?

If I have a few spare minutes, I usually . . . .

If I could do anything I wanted for a whole week, I would love to . . . .

For me the best way to renew my energy and my equilibrium is to . . .

The answers to questions like these can say as much — if not more — about my personality and my physical and psychological needs as about my spirituality. Finding these answers is well worth the effort, since, if I know myself, I can bring my authentic self to prayer, to my relationship with God, the God who lives within me as my loving guest.

~~~~~ II ~~~~~

Mary too was called to a deeper awareness that God was her "guest," the child within her womb. When the Word had become flesh within her, what did she then do? "She rose in haste . . . ." Why did she go to visit her cousin Elizabeth? Mostly because she simply knew that Elizabeth would need her help. Surely she also wanted to rejoice with her cousin at her unexpected pregnancy and to share her own good news with someone who would understand. How did she go? Quickly, joyfully, but probably also with a certain fear, not knowing how it would end. Above all else, she went in faith, believing in God's power to do whatever God wanted, in her and through her. She knew that she carried God within her, and when she embraced Elizabeth, she knew that God's power was in her cousin too.

Try to enter more fully into this mystery: God's respect for Mary's freedom . . . , Mary's faith-filled **yes** to God's request . . . , the all-powerful God enfleshed within her womb . . . , Mary reaching out to her cousin . . . .

Sit with this quietly. Visualize the scenes. Hear the words. Feel the unspoken questions, the deep emotions. Smile with gratitude, with joy. Experience the difficulties and dangers of the journey. Taste Mary's fears, her fatigue. Enter into her complete trust in God's loving plan. Like all of us, Mary was called to be a "contemplative in action." Slowly, very slowly, inhale her peace, her total attention to God within her. Ask for the grace to become more attentive to the God within you.

<div align="center">~~~~~ III ~~~~~</div>

We know from Jesus' words that God is dwelling within us in a way that is just as real as was his presence in Mary's womb. Moreover, each person we encounter in our lives is, in some way, bringing God to us. When we meet this person, we are also being asked to carry God to him or her.

This is what I would call "Visitation spirituality." From the day that Mary's smile touched my heart when I was twenty, this spirituality certainly gave me much peace. It blessed my friendships and enabled me to discover and practice more loving ways to respond to those I found difficult, or who I thought wished me harm. Living this way could make a difference in your relationships too—with others and with God. Being more deeply aware that God is within you and within each person you encounter will help you become a true "contemplative in action."

Picture a few of the people you meet often. No doubt some of these meetings fill you with sheer delight, but others probably cause you varying degrees of stress. Try to imagine how your next encounters with these people might change if you were more conscious of carrying God to them,

and meeting God in them.   Ask confidently for the great
grace of this awareness.

<p align="center">~~~~~ <strong>IV</strong> ~~~~~</p>

Perhaps you have had the privilege of being with
someone you loved as the moment of death approached.   If
so, you know how we cherish their precious last words.   For
me, it was my mother when I was eighteen, and then my
father when I was thirty-one.   These special moments stayed
with me throughout my life.

For all Christians, the words given to us in John,
chapters 15-17, are like Jesus' last will and testament, some
of his most important teachings.   Over and over he tells us
that he wants to live on in us!   He is the vine; we are the
branches.   If we obey his commands, we will remain in his
love, abide in his love.   He will send us the Helper, the Spirit
who comes from the Father.   We will be one with him!   As
in any other loving relationship, our hearts will rejoice,
knowing that we are acting *at God's command and in his
company.*   We will also *see that in our work we can and
ought to witness our gratitude to the God from whom we
have received all things.*

An awareness of this mystery of the Trinity dwelling
within us may well be the most important of our lives.   Take
time to reread these chapters of John and ponder the mystery
of God living within your heart, closer to you than your own
breath.   You may even decide to spend the remaining days
of retreat on the inexhaustible riches of John's words—Jesus'
words.   An entire lifetime would be too short to comprehend
them fully.

For My Guest

In vain I searched the poets' words
        for welcome worthy of my Guest:

Life in whom I live —
        Heart beating beneath my own —
                Someone hidden in this dark with me.

Metaphors leaped and soared,
        but spoke far more than I could feel —
        or less.
Even Scripture: Vine and branches,
        Wind and gentle breeze —
piercing, poignant, living words
        but not yet mine.

Faint streaks of dawn
        broke through the dark
                with silent echoes of my flute.
"Music from the strings no one touches. . ."
        Melodies from the flute no one plays.
                You, you are these melodies!

Will you let me be your flute?
        Warm my wood with your strong hands.
                Blow your breath into my being.
Play your songs through me.
        Our songs will fill some small corner
                of the world —
Songs of double rainbows and ladybugs,
        of broken, shattered dreams.

Let me be your flute.
        Yours the breath, yours the hands,
                ours the melodies!

CLOSING PRAYER

"If you love me, you will obey my commandments.
I will ask the Father, and he will give you another Helper,
who will stay with you forever. This Helper is the Spirit,
who reveals the truth about God. . . .
You know the Helper who is in you and remains with you."
(Jn 14:15-17)

Day 5:

Living God's Dream for Us

In the prayer that Jesus himself taught us, we say, "Thy will be done." How many thousands of times have we prayed these same words! Let us pray them once more, asking for a great desire to live God's loving dream for us.

OPENING PRAYER

A new heart I will give you
and a new spirit I will put within you,
and I will take out of your body the heart of stone
and give you a heart of flesh.
(Ez 36:26)

My wise and wonderful God, thank you for making this promise! Help me to be ready to accept this new spirit, this heart of flesh that you so want to give me.

Help me to see the ways in which I sometimes have a heart of stone, especially in my reactions to others' needs, hardships and misery.

Thank you for the new Spirit you have given me, first at my Baptism, then more and more deeply each time I have received any sacrament or responded to your grace-filled calls.

Help me to envision the ways my life might change if I accept this "heart of flesh," to love you and others with a love that is more giving, more real, more sincere, more passionate.

And thank you for always keeping your promises of mercy!

~~~~~ **I** ~~~~~

Have you ever noticed that throughout the gospels Jesus seems to have one great passion, one driving force? His deepest desire, it seems to me, was to do God's will, to live God's dream. He even called it his 'meat,' the food that kept him going. *If then, we wish to follow God's way of life, a path leading to holiness, we must unite God's counsels and beatitudes to the maxims of the gospel and the instructions of Our Lord. We must follow Jesus along the narrow way, in his poor and humble life.*

To do this presupposes that we know his teachings, his words, "by heart"—as the expression says so well. *The more we follow God without fear, the more will God protect us. The more we do God's will, the more will God prove his love for us!*

If we remind ourselves of the life of Our Lord and that of Our Lady, we will ask ourselves if our lifestyle is characterized by simplicity—*simplicity in our food, our clothing, our rooms, our furniture. For it is in these things that we discover the marvels of God.*

48

Yes, we must really try to *follow Jesus along the narrow way, in his poor and humble life.* What does this mean in the concrete, in our everyday comings and goings? I feel it means, first of all, that we are — as far as we can now see — where God wants us to be, striving to do a good job of whatever our life holds.

Doing this includes practicing what I like to call the "little virtues." *The good God is pleased with little virtues that are practiced for love, and God ennobles them in the measure that they are exercised with greater love. I must do everything, therefore, for the greater love of God.* Everything? Yes, everything. As often as possible, let us be conscious of God's presence within us, as a mother is conscious of her child nearby, and out of pure love, does what is best for the child. These virtues may be little, but they can add up to a magnificent sum, namely, living Gods dream for us!

Can we actually "give" God anything? Everything we are and have is already God's gift to us, yet I am reminded of *a present I gave my father* when I was a child. *It was so small that it made those who saw it laugh, and my father as well. But seeing I had done it with such great affection, he carried this present around with him, and showed it to everyone.*

What might we "give" God today? Perhaps it would simply be the time we spend in prayer — even though that is really God's gift to us! Or perhaps it might be our desire to live God's dream for us as fully as we can. (This, we know, is the only way to be truly happy, both in this life and in the next.) Since this desire is also God's gift to us, let us thank

49

God for it, asking that it may more and more become our passion, our joy, as it was for Jesus!

~~~~~ **III** ~~~~~

Sometimes these "little virtues" take on gigantic proportions, and doing God's will, living God's dream, costs more dearly than we had ever imagined it could. My own purifying trial was almost beyond endurance: for more than four years I felt sure that I was damned. *Even though I could not refuse to recognize my unfortunate state, I never doubted the mercy of God.* When at last, these feelings left me, I was, you may be sure, extremely grateful! I was convinced that there was nothing more for me to do in order to live my gratitude, *than to try to do God's will, to which I had vowed myself long ago.*

Have you ever asked yourself how you really feel about God's dream for you? Do you see it as a barrier that prevents you from enjoying certain pleasures that you would like to have, but that for some reason are not good for you? Or do you see God's dream for you in a more positive light, like the banks of a river that channel the river's energies and keep it from becoming a wide, dangerous swamp? This second way seems wiser, so perhaps you might ask for the grace to grow into a more mature perception of God's will, God's dream for you.

Surely there are some aspects of your present situation that you feel are part of God's dream, but which, in all honesty, you wish could be changed. If they cannot be changed, might they be stepping stones to growth? To what might God be calling you through these challenges? (Someone has said that the way to love everything is to imagine that it might be lost.) What kind of person could truly profit from your situation? Can you pray to become this kind of person? How might you change to become more attuned to God's will, God's loving dream for you?

~~~~~ **IV** ~~~~~

Has anyone ever been as severely tested as Abraham, that dear old nomad whose life was truly a journey in faith? Reread the story in Genesis of his obedience to God's commands, especially as related in chapter 22.

Think back to some of your own difficult moments, when doing God's will seemed beyond your powers—even with God's help! In some way you were being asked to let your precious Isaac (or perhaps your Ishmael?) be taken from you—by others' actions, by your own, or by the inevitable changes of life. Be grateful for whatever response you were able to make at that time, a response which in some way has brought you to this moment of grace.

Pray for others who need strength to continue their daily struggle, perhaps just to survive in lives that are less than human. Say the Our Father for them and their needs, as well as for your own, asking that perhaps through your efforts and actions, God's will for them may be done. Pray with Abraham, our father in faith, that once we know God's will, we will then have the courage to do what God is calling us to do, no matter the cost.

The Way Back

My hand still trembles.
Could I ever have plunged the blade
      into his soft flesh?

Child of promise—
Bravely, like a man, had he carried
      the bundled wood on his small shoulders.
Three days had we trekked
      to reach this barren Moriah.

But mine was the heavier burden:
      live coals, strong cords and this knife,
      its blade flashing like a serpent's tongue.
And then his question—
      and my stumbling response.

Only when I seized his hands to bind them,
      his feet before he could run away,
      did he begin to understand, and accept.

The sheer terror in his eyes!
The disbelief—matched only by my own
      at that terrible command!

Even with my arm raised ready to strike,
      I wonder. . . . Would I have found a way
      to con that strange God as I did at Sodom?
(as I've conned so many others—
      Sarah, Hagar, Abimelich . . .)

But what will he ask of me next?

Come, my son, give me your hand.
      All is well now.

CLOSING PRAYER

You, Lord, give perfect peace to those who keep
their purpose firm
and put their trust in you.
We follow your will and put our hope in you.
You are all that we desire.
(Is 26:3, 8)

'Setting Out'
Sr. Victoire Roy, CND, 1992
Photo C. Riffou, CND
(Marguerite Bourgeoys Museum, Montreal)

Day 6

Loyalty, Fidelity, Honesty

Let's look today at our ability to relate to others. Perhaps our over-dependence needs to mature, or our independence needs to mellow. If we do not know how to nurture our human friendships, our friendship with God will surely suffer.

OPENING PRAYER

"I shall no longer call you servants.
I have called you friends."
(Jn 15:15)

God of surprises and terrible beauty, you call me to live in relationship with others. You do not want me to try to "go it alone,"

but to live an interdependent life
with all its joys and inconveniences.

You allow me to have friends, sometimes very close friends. May my closeness to them never cause me to distance myself from you. And may my human weakness never do them serious injury.

In your human life you felt the delights of relaxing with those who accepted you, the pain of desertion by those you loved, the sorrow of separation when it was time for you, or them, to leave.

Thank you for this precious gift of friendship. May I never take it—or my friends—for granted.

~~~~~ I ~~~~~

If we could change one thing in the people with whom we live and work, what would it be? But should we even try? First of all, considering the many advantages we've had throughout our life and our poor use of some of them, *we ought to believe that our faults are greater and do us more harm than anyone else. Therefore, we must bear with the faults of others so they may bear with us and that God may not condemn us.*

True, others also have their faults. Yet sometimes we *prefer to put up with these faults rather than say something about them, for fear of breaking the peace. Often that is exactly what breaks it!* There are ways to speak assertively without being aggressive. Do we need to look at our options and responsibilities in such situations? To ask for the grace to respond in a nonviolent manner to others' aggression? And let's remember, *God is not satisfied if we preserve the love we owe to others. By our actions we must also preserve others in the love they ought to have for us.* To extend this idea further: How might we improve the way we receive others' love for us? This is a basic aspect of all real relationships, but often goes unnoticed.

Perhaps we also need to look at our way of perceiving others' words and actions that we find hurtful or annoying. A dose of sound psychology can help us respond rather than react in these situations. Pray for light and strength to see and act like Jesus.

~~~~~II ~~~~~

However, we may need to be careful. Some people *would like all to do their duty and become holy—without doing the same themselves. They wish to correct everyone and be corrected by no one. They fill their minds with so many things that they never give themselves the time to think seriously of true and solid virtue.* This retreat may be the time for you to do that, but be careful too not to equate morality with spirituality.

We know that morality is important, of course, since it is our way of expressing our love—or at times, our self-centeredness. But spirituality goes much deeper; it is our relationship with God. To oversimplify, morality is the 'what' of our behavior; spirituality is the 'why.' Some would say that spirituality is our way of seeing, whereas morality is our way of acting. We might say, therefore, that spirituality is the overall framework or vision of our life—encompassing or myopic, grounded or shallow, energetic or lethargic, integrated or fragmented, clear or complicated, focused or haphazard, dynamic or programmed. No matter what else our spirituality may be, it can most certainly be a glorious adventure! I suggest that you pause here and ask for the honesty and humility to see yourself as you are, in all your weakness. But be sure to add with joy and candor, "Dear God, help me to see and believe the truth about myself, no matter how beautiful it may be!"

~~~~~ III ~~~~~

In the light of this faith, pray slowly your favorite psalms, or you might try Psalms 136, 139, 141. Omit or adapt the verses that do not speak your truth, but look well at these verses too—perhaps they do express your feelings more than you care to admit. Be real before our God from whom nothing can be hidden. God knows all before we pray. To omit expressions of anger because they do not seem "proper" in prayer could threaten the real-ness of our relationship with God. To avoid admitting our hostility and even hatred of our enemies makes it impossible to come to the change of heart to which Jesus calls us.

I remember that I once had something of very little value that a good friend was very much interested in. I believed that I should give it to her as a present, but when I had promised it to her, I kept putting off the gift, and so I took away from time to time what was loveliest about it. When I wished to keep my promise, I was repulsed and I lost this person's friendship. Cannot God do the same thing after so many fruitless promises which diminish the value of our gift?

Keeping our promises, nurturing our relationships—both are important aspects of our life. In my own case I could never have survived those turbulent years in Montreal without the support of my two good friends, Jeanne Mance and Governor de Maisonneuve. In fact, there were many times when de Maisonneuve himself came to visit our house simply to seek relief from his trials in hearty laughter! Though we had certainly often sown in tears, we also knew how to sow in mirth too. Nothing very significant, just simple nonsense of little consequence—except to our mental health! These friends were surely God's way of showing me his love in tangible, everyday form, and of giving me

numerous opportunities to grow—of "stretching me."   I
hope you too have such treasures in your life. For most of
us, human friendships are God's love drawing us closer to
himself.

You are surely aware that some people are imbued
with a 'joie de vivre' that puts others at ease. Their gentle
humor—sometimes bizarre but never unkind—spreads
smiles and diffuses tension.   You sense that they are
genuinely happy to be with you, so you can't help but feel
appreciated and special.   They also listen with relaxed
intensity to whatever you say, responding with
understanding, enthusiasm, sympathy or an appropriate
question.

If you are one of these sensitive people who bring
fun and laughter into others' lives, thank God for this gift.
Whatever your gifts, be grateful for them, use them well and
enjoy them all! Finally, you might also consider this: Even
in prayer as we ask for the great gift of contemplation, it's
wise not to take ourselves too seriously. In fact, the ability
to laugh at ourselves (or perhaps, smile gently) may well be
the bedrock of wisdom!

~~~~~**IV** ~~~~~

What about the family God chose for you?   Of
course, it wasn't perfect, but it was one of God's first gifts to
you. Have you taken the time to look back on the ways that
those early years influenced you to become the person you
now are? Have you acknowledged the ways you learned to
cope with the inevitable dysfunctional aspects of those
years? These darker sides of our personality are part of
everyone's story.

And the church, God's own family? Surely you see its weaknesses, as I did in my time. How I struggled with the bishops over certain aspects of our Rule! I tried to remain calm, even in my determination, and to remember that their seeming intransigence was, perhaps, simply due to a different view of what was best for the church, for society or for us.

Are you committed to the church, involved in your parish, loyal to God's community? This concrete involvement will entail working with people of every temperament—not an easy task! In the process you may lose your false freedom—freedom to do as you please, to avoid what irritates you. Your rough edges will be smoothed as you recognize your lack of sensitivity to others' needs. Let us remember that building up the Kingdom of God on earth is a community effort, good people working together.

Have you ever taken the time to look at all that you have received from the church? Why not do it today? Your list will include sources of grace, consolation and inspiration that you may be taking for granted. Perhaps making this list will help you see that even its truly reprehensible aspects might be the reverse-side of something good—or simply part of the human condition. And you may also see ways in which your actions can help the church grow, since we are the church!

His Body

'Mystical' they call his body:
Militant, suffering, triumphant.
Militant? 'Sinful' would say it better.
      We are that body—
      Racist, sexist, stubborn, blind.
      Clamoring to kill those who kill.
Killing for oil and our way of life.
Stealing from those who have nothing.
Wallowing in arrogance, living a lie.
      Infecting spouse and children with death.
      Sowing hatred, reaping wealth.
Selling guns to brother slaughtering brother.
Planting land mines to murder and maim.
Mocking the sacred, shattering vows.

Expecting forgiveness, refusing pardon.
Turning away from haunting eyes,
      outstretched hands.

His body—scourged, bleeding, leprous—
      Doctors dismembering babies limb by limb.
Judges deciding the legality of this 'procedure.'
Most of us too busy to cry out in horror and rage!

Yet I feel his pleading eyes: Will you also go away?
      This body is all I have—this ugliness
      suffused with light.

CLOSING PRAYER

Create a pure heart in me, O God, and put a new
and loyal spirit in me.
Give me again the joy that comes from your salvation,
and make me willing to obey you.
Sincerity and truth are what you require;
fill my mind with your wisdom.
(Ps 51:10, 12, 6)

Day 7

Enfolded in God's Mercy

Today we will look at the weakness that is part of the human condition. Only when we know that we are enfolded in God's loving arms can we safely look at ourselves as we really are—sinners, yes, but sinners whom Jesus loves so much that, if necessary, he would die again to save.

OPENING PRAYER

"People who are well do not need a doctor, but only those who are sick." (Mt 9:3)

Compassionate and passionate God, thank you for the many times you have come to heal me—

. . . to heal me of my sins through sorrow and confession,
. . . to heal me of my fears and doubts through others' confidence in me,
. . . to heal me of my pride by allowing me to make mistakes,
. . . to heal me of my selfishness by sending the needy to my door,
. . . to heal me of my coldness by allowing me to love another deeply and be loved in return,

. . . to heal my restless heart of its hungers by feeding me
with the Bread of Life,
. . . to heal me of my anger and resentment by touching me
through another's patient caring.

Help me always to see your loving hand behind whatever
medicine life prescribes for me, so that little by little I may
be completely healed of whatever is keeping me from being
all that you want me to be. Help me too, divine Physician,
to be wise enough to exercise every day—to exercise the
virtues that you call me to practice in my daily encounters
with others.

~~~~~ I ~~~~~

In looking back over our lives, we are sure to see a
long list of mistakes, faults, sins. Yet look again! For each
of these, if we're honest, we're bound to see that God drew
something good from it—either because of this very sin or
in spite of it. Who else but God could do this? This is
surely omnipotence!

Can you take the time today to see the darker parts of
your life in this light? To praise the power of God for his
merciful love? You could adapt Psalm 136 to your story,
and after each part, repeat with joy a refrain such as, "For
God's great love and mercy are truly without end!"

In my own life and in everyone else's, *I never
doubted the mercy of God.* I knew that I would *always
hope in God, even if I saw myself with one foot in hell.* To
be honest, we must admit that *a careless, lax and easy life is
a dense cloud which hides from our eyes the boundless
treasure of his goodness.* These days of quiet prayer are a
time of grace. Ask God to break through whatever clouds

surround you, with the light and warmth of his sun, so you can see your life in a new way, and see yourself as God sees you—with infinite delight in you as you are now! On what do we base our unshakable trust? *On the merits of the precious blood given for our ransom!*

<center>~~~~~ II ~~~~~</center>

Jesus tried so hard to make us see God's boundless love for us. Perhaps his most passionate story is that of the prodigal son (Lk 15. 11-32). In subtle ways (or maybe not so subtle) the prodigal son lives on in each of us—as does his elder brother. You may wish to allow these two parts of you to dialogue about your life—past or present, then listen to the Father receiving you both, and feel him embracing you both.

If you can arrange to receive the Sacrament of Reconciliation, I hope you will do so. Know that your own joy and peace at receiving God's healing pardon are as nothing compared to the Father's infinite joy at what you are giving him in allowing him to bestow this gift on you, his prodigal daughter or son, and on the elder brother too!

Throughout his ministry Jesus embodied the Father's merciful love for humankind. When we read the gospels carefully, however, we see that he had a predilection for certain kinds of people, namely, the poor and the sinful. Surely, we are included among those whom our Good Shepherd searches for, finds, and carries home in his arms. In the special prayer he taught us, he told us to ask for mercy, for forgiveness. But note the condition that we attach to our request: Give us mercy in the measure we give it to others!

~~~~~ **III** ~~~~~

Over and over in his teachings and parables, Jesus reminds us that we must show mercy, forgiveness and kindness to others.

Consider the following passages:

Lk 10:25-37:   The Good Samaritan, with its clear command at the end: "Go, and do the same yourself."

Mt 25:31-46: The Last Judgment, which shows that the blessed of God are those who have practiced charity in their actions.

Mt 18:23-35:   The Unforgiving Debtor, which explicitly teaches that forgiveness on our part is essential if we wish to receive God's mercy. "Were you not bound to have pity on your fellow servant as I had pity on you?"

If we are truly aware of being enfolded in God's mercy, we will show this in our own merciful attitudes, forgiving others from our heart. *If we follow the way of divine wisdom, we will forgive the other's intention whenever we cannot excuse the fault itself.* This mercy will then spill over into our actions—pity and compassion for those who need our help, both material and spiritual.

Ponder one or more of these parables, then with trustful persistence ask for a deeper awareness of God's mercy. Pray that you may become more compassionate in your whole being—your attitudes, speech, tone of voice, gestures and actions.

In the fifth Beatitude we see again that only if we are merciful will we receive God's mercy. This forgiving love for others is fundamental to all the other Beatitudes. It means going out of ourselves to respond to our neighbor who is in need, overcoming our self-centeredness in order to reach out to others. Beg for the grace to see that the only fitting response to God's boundless mercy is to share the gift of forgiveness with others. Ask God to show you who these "others" are and how you might become more God-like, more merciful.

We know that today more than ever before peoples of poor nations, minorities in our own country, and even the earth itself—all are crying out for mercy. Take some time to listen to these cries, and to pray about how you might personally respond to God's call to you through their voices.

You might also wish to ponder Hosea's love for Gomer (Hos. Ch. 1-3) and feel God's merciful love for you.

Return

Yes, I have heard you, Hosea.
No longer will I seek my lovers
        nor claim your gifts as theirs—
        warm wool and linen,
        silver squandered like sand,
        incense burned before Baal.
You have bought me dearly,
        brought me back to our table
        and made me listen to your silence.

We are together as of old, my husband,
        just you and I.

You take my hands in yours.
        I feel your breath on my palms.
Dare I look into your eyes?

Hosea, they brim with tears!
Before I can speak my sorrow,
        you pour out yours—
        pain for the pain that fills my being,
        for my body, weakened and worn,
        for my heart, breaking with shame.
Your tears tell your love.
        Your heart knows my love.
        The earth throbs with our love
        as once again we are one.

CLOSING PRAYER

The Lord's unfailing love and mercy still continue,
fresh as the morning, sure as the sunrise.
The Lord is all I have, and so in God I put my hope.
(Lam 3:22-24)

AFTERWORD

So now your retreat is finished. Yet in a sense, is it ever finished? In fact, it may just be beginning. You have met a seventeenth-century woman whose life has become intertwined with your own. She has become your friend, a friend who will forever be interested in you.

Perhaps you have come to realize that you are being loved into wholeness, completely and unconditionally. It may be that God has spoken to you in a new way, helping you become aware of his living presence within you. You may have drawn near to Mary and seen her in a new light. She may have spoken to you as to Marguerite, "Go, I will never abandon you!"

God may have touched your heart through Scripture and allowed you to see Jesus reaching out to heal the pain around him, your pain and mine. Jesus' burning desire for peace and justice for all people on this earth may have come alive for you.

Perhaps these days were simple days of quiet, with no unusual insights. Or there may have been tension, or darkness, but even here, God was in the 'desert' with you, keeping you safe in his arms.

You may wish to remember some of these moments, to hold on to them so that they do not slip away with the passing of time. How to do this? You might decide to reread your retreat notes—or whatever you may have written—occasionally, perhaps once a month. Or you could reopen this book periodically, and ponder again the passages you may have marked as significant for you.

Sometimes the writing process itself can sharpen our insights—as well as help us recall them later. As this time of retreat comes to a close, you might ponder the following sentence, finishing it in your own way, then put your thoughts into writing: "A Christian today is a person who...."

As a logical corollary, you might then continue: "Perhaps God is now inviting me to deepen or change some aspect of my life. To fulfill God's loving dream for me more completely, I might try to...." Whatever you decide on (and choose to write), it's wise to keep it 'do-able.'

Remember that you are deeply loved, and always will be. Being human is a graced privilege beyond our wildest dreams. With Marguerite, may you live your life passionately, in ever deeper joy and compassion!

Amen! Alleluia! Amen!

Part Three

More about Marguerite

A. Bibliography:

The following are some of the books in English available from:

> *Marguerite Bourgeoys Museum*
> *400 Saint Paul St. East*
> *Montreal, QC H2Y 1H4*
> *Canada*

Bourgeoys, Marguerite. *The Writings of Marguerite Bourgeoys*. Montreal: Congregation de Notre Dame 1976.

Charron, Yvon, PSS. *Mother Bourgeoys*. Montreal: Beauchemin 1950.

Glandelet, Charles de. *The True Spirit*. Compiled 1700-1701. Montreal: Congregation de Notre Dame 1977.

Poissant, Simone, CND. *Marguerite Bourgeoys 1620-1700,* 2nd edition (Translated by Frances Kirwan, CND). Montreal: Bellarmin 1993.

Simpson, Patricia, CND. *Marguerite Bourgeoys and Montreal, 1640-1665.* Montreal: McGill-Queen's University Press 1997.*

Simpson, Patricia, CND. *Marguerite Bourgeoys and the Congregation of Notre Dame, 1665-1700.* Montreal: McGill-Queen's University Press 2006.*

These last two books are written in a lively, flowing style. The result of years of careful research, they are considered the definitive biography of Marguerite Bourgeoys. In her extensive bibliographies, the author cites numerous other books and articles about Marguerite Bourgeoys, early Montreal, seventeenth-century religious life, etc. (in both French and English).

Also available are illustrated books about Marguerite Bourgeoys for children of all ages.

B. Music: "VISITATION" (CD)

Tracks:

1. Mary's Alleluia*
2. Morning Song*
3. Simple Gifts*
4. All that I Have Ever Desired*
5. Song of the Disciple*
6. Prayer of the Congregation*
7. The Queen's Song*
8. In the Footsteps of Mary+
9. Mission Song*
10. The More I Follow*
11. Living Water*
12. Psalm of the Beloved*
13. I Want to Feel Little*
14. Almighty God*
15. Spirit of Charity*
16. Blessing Song*
17. Be Always Little+
18. Visitation Song+
19. Magnificat+
20. Ave Maria*

All Songs ©1999
*Kathleen Deignan, CND and +Mary Anne Foley, CND

Schola Ministries
4301 Connecticut Ave. NW – Suite 404
Washington, DC 20008-2369
(202) 237-1286 - - 1-866-620-1286
kdeignan@scholaministries.org

C. Illustrations:

Throughout this text a variety of portraits of Marguerite have been added as a possible aid to prayer. Obviously, none is an actual photograph. Since Marguerite's death, many artists have tried to give her a countenance, an appearance—in drawings, paintings, engravings, sculpture. An example of one such engraving can be found on Page 7. They tried to be faithful to seventeenth century history, to inherited documents and accounts. Each generation of artists also tried to reflect the language and spirituality of their own time, in order to illumine the face of Marguerite for their contemporaries. For most of the works included in this book, the identifications accompanying the picture are sufficient.

The final portrait, however, needs a further explanation of its intriguing history. This story will also shed light on the portrait called, 'The Pseudo-Le Ber,' found on page 39. For this, I have drawn heavily on two sources, and I am grateful to Sr. Danielle Dubois, CND and Sr. Patricia Simpson, CND for their broad research and fresh insights.[1]

In religious art, the goal of the artist is to reveal through the visible the mystery of the invisible. So it was in 1700, when Pierre Le Ber studied Marguerite's face as she lay in her coffin. Talented though untrained, he quickly painted the woman he had known from his earliest years. His brush captured more than her features. Even in death, he saw her as practical, kind, decisive, intelligent, peaceful and energetic. To him this was her inner beauty, far more important than her aged reality.

One scholar suggests that within a generation, however, the sisters of the Congregation (perhaps influenced by others in Montreal) wanted a portrait of Marguerite that would be less 'realistic' and more attractive.[2] Their desire was granted. A drawing or miniature of a serene young woman, clearly modeled on Le Ber's portrait, in turn became the model for many other paintings during the next century or more. (An example of one of these may be seen on p. 7.) This practice of copying previous works was common at the time, when religious art was expected to be edifying and respectful of tradition. Even Le Ber's painting was retouched and 'improved' several times, until, finally, one of these more pleasing portraits was considered the original—a misconception that continued for more than a century. (This portrait is now referred to as 'the Pseudo-Le Ber.')

By the early 1960s many suspected that another completely different painting might still exist underneath the various layers of retouching. As the investigations continued, a professional restorer in New York, Edward O. Korany, was engaged to restore—if possible—the original. After a copy of the pseudo-Le Ber was made, Korany began the delicate work of removing the upper layers and uncovering the original. He knew nothing about the person in the painting, except that she was a seventeenth-century religious figure.

After several months of painstaking labor, his work was successfully completed. The original portrait was intact! "When asked for his first reaction to the face he had revealed, he answered with one word, 'Compassion'.[3]

Clearly "Le Ber's portrait is that not of an idealized saint already enjoying the beatific vision, but that of an old woman who carries on her face the marks of much suffering."[4]

Especially in today's culture, with its constant emphasis on physical beauty and youthful vigor, many of us are not able to relate to such stark realism. Our preference tends towards softer, less austere, more pleasing lines. If so, we wisely choose other visuals of Marguerite that we find more helpful to our prayer and to our relationship with her.

Danielle Dubois reminds us that "a true work of religious art does not give answers but asks questions, speaks more of absence than of certitude. . . ."[5] Perhaps this 'True Likeness' (found on page 83) will speak to you of Marguerite's immense desire for God. Perhaps it will draw you further and further into a Love story that fills you with life, with challenges and questions. If so, ponder it in prayer, live with the questions, accept the absence of certitude—as Marguerite did in her own life.

Finally, on a lighter note, it might be of interest to know that the French word for 'daisy' is 'marguerite.' Thus, the addition of several of these flowers throughout the text.

[1] Dubois, Danielle, CND, "From Sight to Insight," (pp. 4-8) *Courrier Marguerite-Bourgeoys, No. 53, 1994*; Simpson, Patricia, CND, *Marguerite Bourgeoys and the Congregation of Notre-Dame 1665-1700, pp. 215-234.*
[2] Alfred Morin, quoted in "The Likeness of Marguerite Bourgeoys," p. 11, *Courrier Marguerite-Bourgeoys, No. 53, 1994.*
[3] Simpson, p. 229.
[4] Simpson, p. 232.
[5] Dubois, p. 8.

'Marguerite Bourgeoys and the Children'
by Sr. St. Renée LaChance, 1904
(Marguerite Bourgeoys Museum, Montreal)

77

D. Through a Poet's Eyes:

Several poets have also tried to capture Marguerite's spirit in their verbal imagery—an impossible task, but like all such, a labor of love. The following is one of my own efforts (1982).

. . . One Gift More

You walk with us
in dangers sensed
and unsuspected in the dark
beyond the known, approved, expected,
to find him in the drumbeats of a dream.

With you we turn to continents uncharted
in hovels, hollows, wasteland suburbs,
to troubled, voiceless, shackled minds
to broken spirits,
haunted, hollow eyes
with shrinking hopes spinning to their doom.

You walk with us
on paths outside the fort of safe success.
Peace-bearers,
we place another cross
against the messages of ignorance and fear.
A broken cannon, now a bell,
recalls us to the chapel of our truth.
With you we follow Mary
in company with Christ,
not in austerity or constant contemplation
(where once you too felt drawn)
but in simple journeys—
each day a Visitation

where women bring the dawn
in song and grateful praise,
where hidden service frees
for future greatness,
where new life greets our own
in joy!

Your steps (wise mother!) are child-small
inviting us to shed our hard-won wisdom
and grow to littleness.

We laugh—
an echo of your own
with friends of early years—
Jeanne Mance or faithful Paul.

What else but laugh
at memories of salt-sprayed sleep
pillowed on a coil of rope?

How else survive the birthpangs
of a colony
but laugh and pray
and shrug your shoulders?

How else convince
our News is truly Good
except with joy?

More than taffy on the path
brought children to your door!
Solid fare—bread and soup—well seasoned
with wit, lively or profound,
nourished hungers of the spirit too.
You shared the recipe with all who asked.
Mending, baking, scrubbing, soothing—

no task too big or small for mother-hands.
A mattress or a remedy, a handclasp or a hug—
you sensed the need and gave.
Truly present to the gentle and the grumbling,
the laughter, triumphs, dry tears of others,
may we too listen,
and respond.

Our stable walls have stretched
in welcome to a family unforeseen:
to daughters of the King, and sons,
the young with eager questions
and not-so-young with hardened answers,
to children of the plains and parish,
the ghettos and the mines.

You pray
that we will shine with clarity undimmed,
wick cleaned, oil purified,
aglow with his presence,
afire with his love,
pierced with its passion—
a lavish, foolish, playful, lover's love!

You pray with us
to let him be our soil, moisture, seed,
to let him warm us with his morning shade,
unfolding petals
perfect in their brief brightness.

Your prayer persists
in vigil by our scanty store
till strong spring ships arrive
with new flour
for the Bread we share.

You speak.
    We listen gladly.
Be always little,
like cabbages and pumpkins—
    Yes! To him the glory!
and humble,
at home with shepherds and kings—
    To him the praise!
and poor.
    Poor?
    Unsafe! Unwise!
    Our culture's changed—

Be poor in food and clothes.
Be poor in housing too.
    But how?
    Our works—his works—
    demand . . . 'a certain standard.'
At his command I came,
a bundle on my back.
    Our needs have grown.
Their tendrils choke your freedom.
Be poor.

Pity our weakness.
Pity our chains.
Pity our part with tyrants' guilt
who strip and starve his other children
and smiling, turn away.
Give us your eyes
to see the chasm of our nothingness.
Come closer, you say.
Groping blindly, we balance on the brink,
emptied, despoiled of all—
all but trust.
Then, swallowed by the depths of dizzying truth,

we fall.
Past destitution.
Past rejection, pain, pleas for pardon.
Past burning hunger for his Will.
Finally, we feel another darkness,
a limitless abyss far deeper
than the misery of stark need, or creature-poverty—
a Father's mercy, a Mother's love.

Marguerite,
in us you live your vision.
Through us you touch our world.

You've given us another family!
You've taught us well.
You've shown us when to lay aside
our dream
and waken to another's.

But one gift more
surpasses all the rest:
Mary, our guide,
Mary, our life.
We feel her smile
and bow in wordless wonder,
then, arms flung wide, we run to her embrace.

Marguerite,
when layered years
are gently scraped away,
may your compassion be complete
in us—
in likeness to our mother,
    sister,
    friend.

'The True Likeness'
Painting of Marguerite Bourgeoys
by Pierre LeBer, 1700
(Marguerite Bourgeoys Museum, Montreal)

Called to Compassion is a book to read and pray. Within the framework of seven prayer-days, the author gently weaves together strands of spirituality, Scripture, psychology and common sense. Each day's offerings are drawn from the writings of a seventeenth-century contemplative in action whose message is timeless. Divided into four prayer-periods per day, Saint Marguerite Bourgeoys' words come alive as she 'speaks' to the reader in clear, cogent prose, punctuated by poetic insights.

Marguerite Bourgeoys left her native France as a young single woman to join with other committed lay persons in a wonderful adventure. With the gospel journey of Mary to Elizabeth as her model, Marguerite founded an uncloistered community of women to meet the educational needs of her time. That Congregation has endured for over 300 years.

– Sr. Patricia McCarthy, CND

Sr. Louise Finn, CND, a member of the Congregation of Notre Dame, has been a lifelong teacher and administrator. Nearly half of her fifty-plus years of ministry have been on the Pine Ridge Reservation in South Dakota and at a seminary in Cameroon, Africa. Presently, she is librarian at an inner-city Nativity school in New Haven, Connecticut.